JALEN HURTS

SPORTS SUPERSTARS

BY THOMAS K. ADAMSON

BELLWETHER MEDIA • MINNEAPOLIS, MN

Torque brims with excitement perfect for thrill-seekers of all kinds. Discover daring survival skills, explore uncharted worlds, and marvel at mighty engines and extreme sports. In *Torque* books, anything can happen. Are you ready?

This edition first published in 2024 by Bellwether Media, Inc.

No part of this publication may be reproduced in whole or in part without written permission of the publisher. For information regarding permission, write to Bellwether Media, Inc., Attention: Permissions Department, 6012 Blue Circle Drive, Minnetonka, MN 55343.

Library of Congress Cataloging-in-Publication Data

LC record for Jalen Hurts available at: https://lccn.loc.gov/2023040020

Text copyright © 2024 by Bellwether Media, Inc. TORQUE and associated logos are trademarks and/or registered trademarks of Bellwether Media, Inc.

Editor: Kieran Downs   Designer: Gabriel Hilger

Printed in the United States of America, North Mankato, MN.

TABLE OF CONTENTS

PLAYOFF POWER RUN	4
WHO IS JALEN HURTS?	6
COLLEGE CHALLENGES	8
A TALENTED LEADER	14
A BRIGHT FUTURE	20
GLOSSARY	22
TO LEARN MORE	23
INDEX	24

PLAYOFF POWER RUN

The Philadelphia Eagles lead the San Francisco 49ers in the 2022 **conference championship game**. The Eagles have the ball on the 1-yard line.

Eagles **quarterback** Jalen Hurts takes the ball. He pushes in for the **touchdown**! The Eagles go on to win. They are headed to **Super Bowl** 57!

2022 NFC CHAMPION

WHO IS JALEN HURTS?

Jalen Hurts is a quarterback in the **National Football League** (NFL). He led the Eagles to the Super Bowl in only his third season.

JALEN HURTS

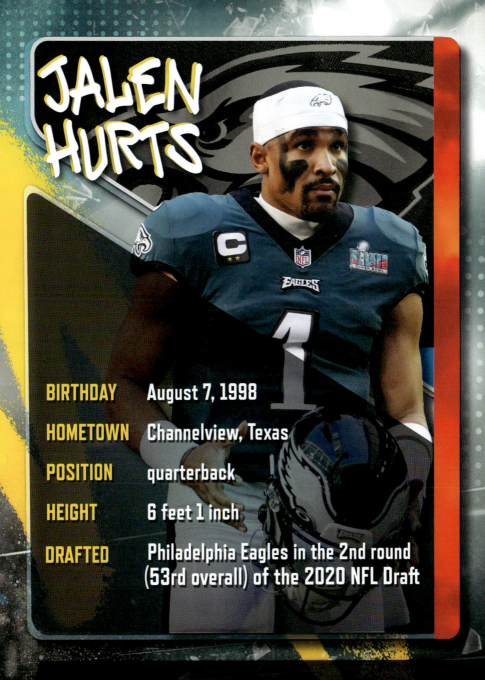

BIRTHDAY August 7, 1998

HOMETOWN Channelview, Texas

POSITION quarterback

HEIGHT 6 feet 1 inch

DRAFTED Philadelphia Eagles in the 2nd round (53rd overall) of the 2020 NFL Draft

Hurts is known as both a strong passer and a powerful runner. He is also known for being a good leader.

COLLEGE CHALLENGES

Football was always a big part of Hurts's life. His dad was his high school coach. Hurts learned from his parents to work hard and never give up.

Fast and Strong

Hurts ran track in high school. He was also in powerlifting. Powerlifting is a sport in which people try to lift more weight than others.

Hurts went to college at the University of Alabama. In his first year, he was named the Southeastern Conference (SEC) **Offensive** Player of the Year.

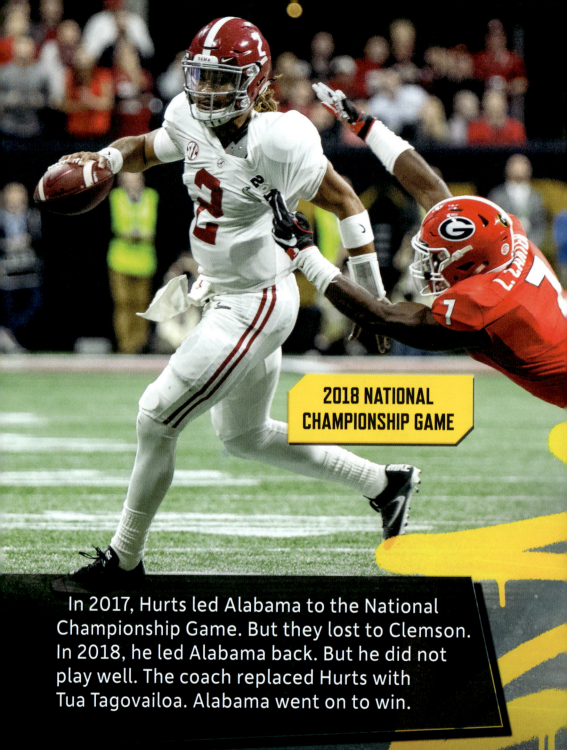

2018 NATIONAL CHAMPIONSHIP GAME

In 2017, Hurts led Alabama to the National Championship Game. But they lost to Clemson. In 2018, he led Alabama back. But he did not play well. The coach replaced Hurts with Tua Tagovailoa. Alabama went on to win.

Hurts was shaken by being benched in the biggest game of his life. Tagovailoa was named the starter the next year.

TUA TAGOVAILOA

JALEN HURTS

In late 2018, Alabama played Georgia in the SEC championship game. Late in the game, Tagovailoa was hurt. Hurts replaced him and led the team in a comeback win. But Tagovailoa remained the starter for the rest of the season.

In 2019, Hurts left Alabama for the University of Oklahoma. That season, Hurts finished second in voting for the **Heisman Trophy**.

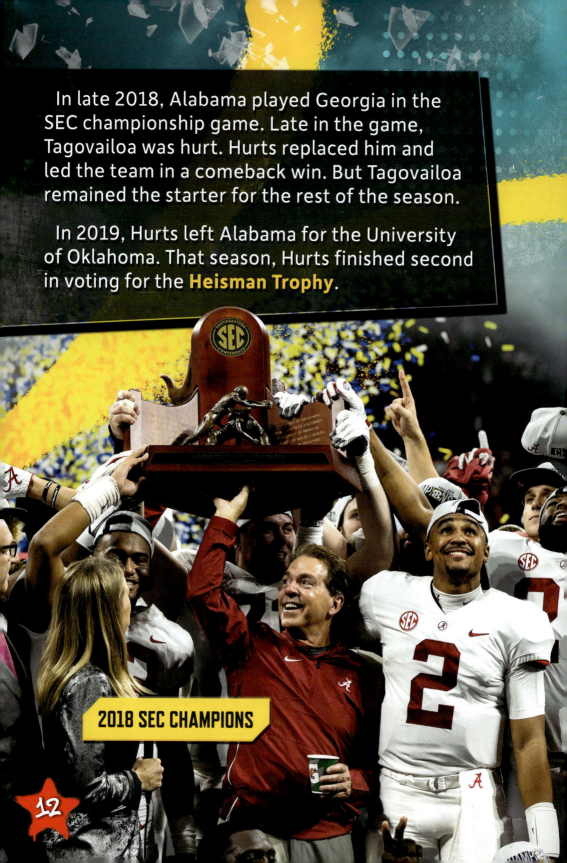

2018 SEC CHAMPIONS

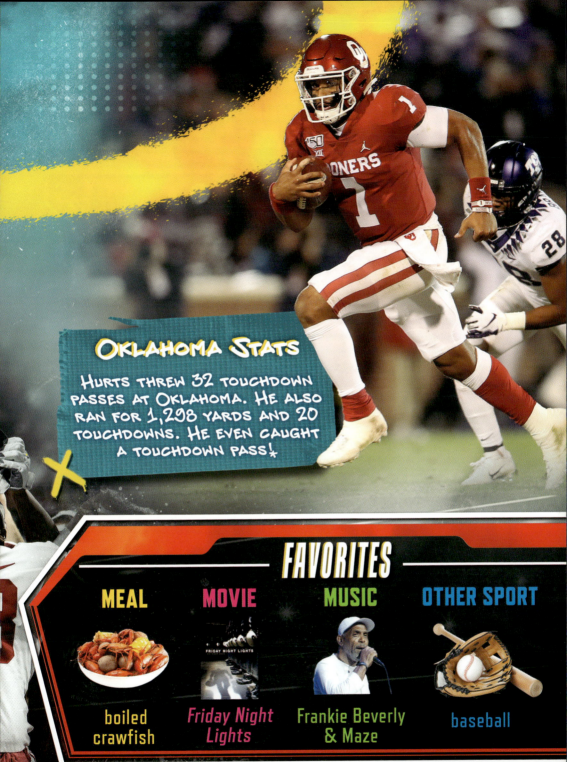

Oklahoma Stats

Hurts threw 32 touchdown passes at Oklahoma. He also ran for 1,298 yards and 20 touchdowns. He even caught a touchdown pass!*

FAVORITES

MEAL
boiled crawfish

MOVIE
Friday Night Lights

MUSIC
Frankie Beverly & Maze

OTHER SPORT
baseball

A TALENTED LEADER

The Eagles **drafted** Hurts in the second round of the 2020 NFL Draft. But the Eagles already had a starting quarterback in Carson Wentz.

That season, Wentz struggled. Hurts became the starting quarterback late in the season. In his first game as a starter, he led the team to a win over the New Orleans Saints.

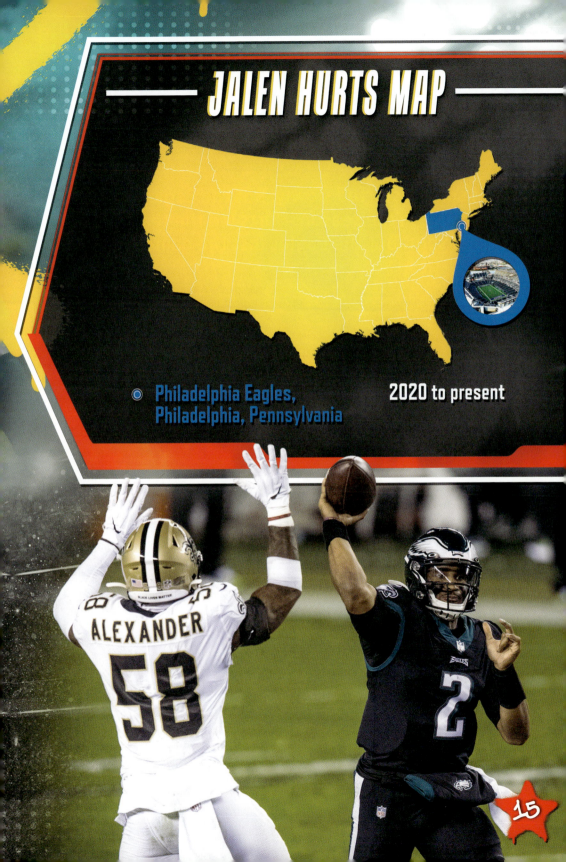

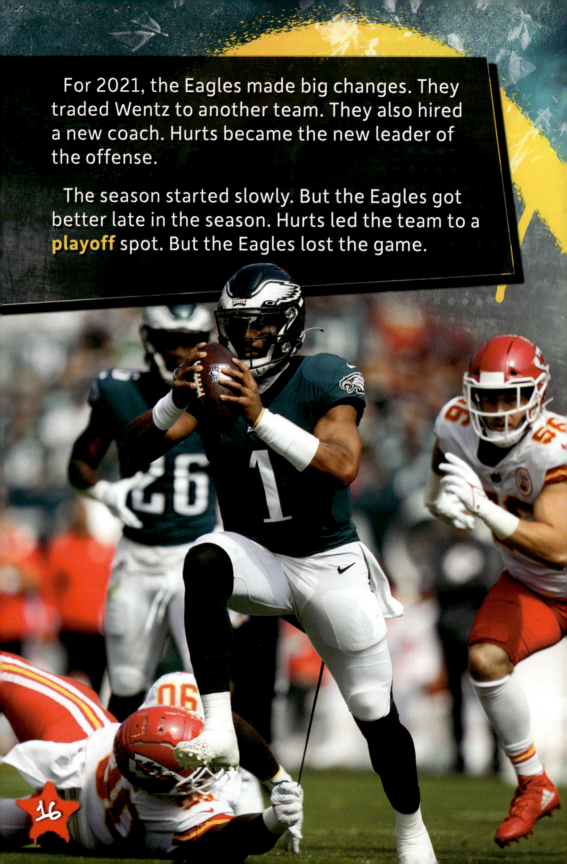

For 2021, the Eagles made big changes. They traded Wentz to another team. They also hired a new coach. Hurts became the new leader of the offense.

The season started slowly. But the Eagles got better late in the season. Hurts led the team to a **playoff** spot. But the Eagles lost the game.

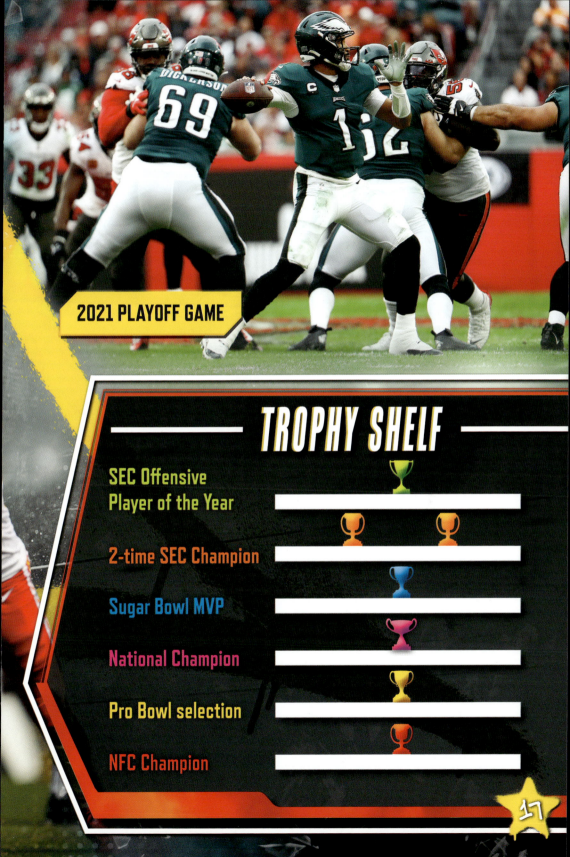

2021 PLAYOFF GAME

TROPHY SHELF

- SEC Offensive Player of the Year
- 2-time SEC Champion
- Sugar Bowl MVP
- National Champion
- Pro Bowl selection
- NFC Champion

In 2022, Hurts had an amazing season. He passed for 3,701 yards. He ran for 13 touchdowns. The Eagles won 14 games. Hurts came in second in **Most Valuable Player** (MVP) voting. He was selected to the **Pro Bowl**.

Hurts led the Eagles to Super Bowl 57. But they lost a close game to the Chiefs.

TIMELINE

— 2018 —
Hurts is benched by Alabama in the National Championship Game

— 2019 —
Hurts leaves Alabama and joins Oklahoma

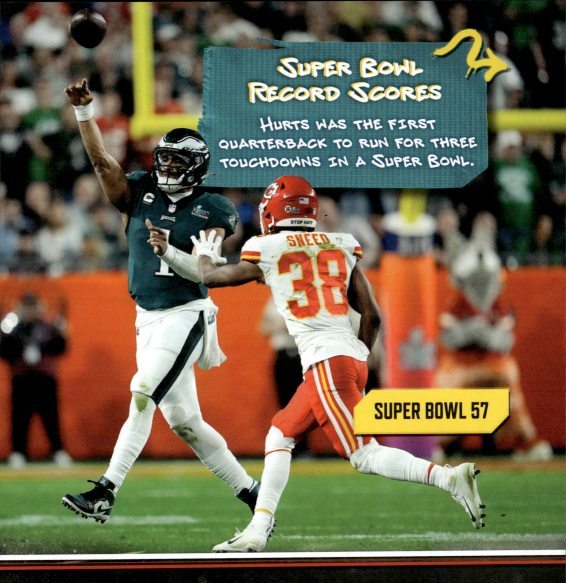

Super Bowl Record Scores

Hurts was the first quarterback to run for three touchdowns in a Super Bowl.

SUPER BOWL 57

— 2020 —
Hurts is drafted by the Eagles

— February 2023 —
The Eagles play in Super Bowl 57

— April 2023 —
Hurts agrees to play with the Eagles for five more years

A BRIGHT FUTURE

Hurts knows that people look up to him. He wants to play hard and be respectful. Hurts also gives back to the community. He works with a program that helps kids in Philadelphia.

Hurts keeps working to improve. Before the 2023 season, Hurts agreed to play with the Eagles for at least five more years. He wants to win a Super Bowl with the Eagles!

GLOSSARY

conference championship game—a contest to decide the best team or person

drafted—chose by a process where professional teams choose high school and college athletes to play for them

Heisman Trophy—an award that goes to the best college football player of the season

Most Valuable Player—the best player in a year, game, or series; the most valuable player is often called the MVP.

National Football League—a professional football league in the United States; the National Football League is often called the NFL.

offensive—related to players who have the ball and are trying to score

playoff—related to games played after the regular season is over; playoff games determine which teams play in the championship game.

Pro Bowl—a game between the best players in the National Football League

quarterback—a player on offense whose main job is to throw and hand off the ball

Super Bowl—the annual championship game for the National Football League

touchdown—a score that occurs when a team crosses into their opponent's end zone with the football; a touchdown is worth six points.

TO LEARN MORE

AT THE LIBRARY

Doeden, Matt. *Meet Jalen Hurts: Philadelphia Eagles Superstar*. Minneapolis, Minn.: Lerner Publications, 2024.

Klepeis, Alicia Z. *The Philadelphia Eagles*. Minneapolis, Minn.: Bellwether Media, 2024.

Smith, Elliott. *Football's Greatest Myths and Legends*. North Mankato, Minn.: Capstone Press, 2023.

ON THE WEB

Factsurfer.com gives you a safe, fun way to find more information.

1. Go to www.factsurfer.com

2. Enter "Jalen Hurts" into the search box and click 🔍.

3. Select your book cover to see a list of related content.

INDEX

awards, 4, 9, 12
championship, 4, 10, 12
childhood, 8
drafted, 14
family, 8
favorites, 13
future, 21
Heisman Trophy, 12
map, 15
Most Valuable Player, 18
National Football League, 6, 14
Offensive Player of the Year, 9
Philadelphia Eagles, 4, 6, 14, 16, 18, 21
playoff, 16, 17
Pro Bowl, 18
profile, 7
quarterback, 4, 6, 14, 19
record, 19
Southeastern Conference, 9, 12
stats, 13
Super Bowl, 4, 6, 18, 19, 21
Tagovailoa, Tua, 10, 11, 12
timeline, 18–19
touchdown, 4, 13, 18, 19
trophy shelf, 17
University of Alabama, 9, 10, 12
University of Oklahoma, 12, 13
Wentz, Carson, 14, 16

The images in this book are reproduced through the courtesy of: Rich Schultz, AP Newsroom, front cover; ZUMA Press, Inc./ Alamy, p. 3; Matt Slocum/ AP Images/ AP Newsroom, pp. 4, 16, 18-19; Matt Rourke/ AP Images/ AP Newsroom, pp. 4-5; Winslow Townson/ AP Images/ AP Newsroom, p. 6; Cooper Neill/ AP Images/ AP Newsroom, pp. 7 (Jalen Hurts), 23; Jeff Bukowski, p. 7 (Eagles logo); Tony Gutierrez/ AP Images/ AP Newsroom, p. 8; Tim Warner/ AP Images/ AP Newsroom, p. 9; Scott Kinser/ AP Images/ AP Newsroom, p. 10; Logan Bowles/ AP Images/ AP Newsroom, p. 11; Ric Tapia/ AP Images/ AP Newsroom, p. 12; David Stacy/Icon Sportswire/ AP Images/ AP Newsroom, p. 13 (Jalen Hurts); P Maxwell Photography, p. 13 (boiled crawfish); AJ Pics/ Alamy, p. 13 (*Friday Night Lights*); Mel E Brown, p. 13 (Frankie Beverly & Maze); Andrey_Popov, p. 13 (baseball); Matt Ludtke/ AP Images/ AP Newsroom, p. 14; Brian E Kushner, p. 15 (Eagles stadium); Albert Tielemans/ AP Images/ AP Newsroom, p. 15 (Jalen Hurts); Kevin Sabitus/ AP Images/ AP Newsroom, p. 17; Chris Szagola/ AP Images/ AP Newsroom, pp. 18 (Jalen Hurts), 20; University of Alabama/ Wiki Commons, p. 18 (Alabama Crimson Tide logo); University of Oklahoma/ Wiki Commons, p. 18 (Oklahoma Sooners logo); NFL/ Wiki Commons, p. 19 (Eagles logo); Derik Hamilton/ AP Images/ AP Newsroom, p. 21.